WAWEL

WAWEL

Adam Bujak

Text **JAN K. OSTROWSKI**

 Biały Kruk

The Royal Wawel

It is impossible to miss. Entering the city or roaming its streets, squares and residential areas you will see it in ever changing shapes and angles. The Wawel silhouette continues to constitute an integral part of the Cracow cityscape, though so much has been done to turn the thousand year old city into a cluster of boxy and grey concrete housing blocks, their monotony interrupted by factory stacks, rather than church towers. Each one of these chance glimpses of the Wawel, in their diversity and a pleasant sort of disarray, affords a fresh impression every time. Some of them are particularly worth recommending.

Take a look from the west, from across the Vistula River, or perhaps from the Dębnicki Bridge. Below you will see the bend of the Vistula with white limestone cliffs hiding the Dragon's Den above. Still higher, the dark red fortress walls supporting red and white stretch of old capitular and seminary buildings, incorporating fragments of medieval fortifications. The view is crowned with towers and spires of the Cathedral and the Thieves' Tower. You cannot help but notice the heavy bulk of an old Austrian hospital as well. This is unfortunate, but not everything that history has bestowed on the Wawel may be a source of pride. An eastern view from Stradom Street presents a section of genuine Gothic Wawel with a slim oriel of the Hen's Foot, the Danish Tower – its facade covered with elegant stone fluting – and with the Senators' Tower closing the vista off from the left.

It requires some more effort to find a convenient viewing spot from the north. It would be best to take a walk along the Planty park or through the garden of the Archaeological Museum located in the former Carmelite Monastery. Seen from this side, the Castle appears rather undifferentiated. However, the exquisite Cathedral, together with its separate Treasury building and impressive towers, appears at its best. Seen below are the Austrian fortress walls, and the old course way leading from the outlet of Kanonicza Street to the top of the Hill along a wall studded with memorial briquettes. Southern view would be the hardest to come by. It would be necessary to climb up to the terrace of the Krzemionki, or even up to the TV broadcast tower.

This is definitely worth the effort, for in return you are rewarded not only with an unsurpassed view of the silhouette of the Cathedral with the golden kernel of the Sigismund Chapel, but also of the rich aura of the churches in Kazimierz, framing of Wawel Hill in the foreground.

Wawel's multifold vistas took centuries to shape. To understand their unique shape one has to know at least a handful of facts concerning the history of Wawel Hill and the buildings erected on it, which also happen to constitute a considerable part of the nation's history.

* * *

Over a thousand years ago, at the dawn of documented Wawel history, the area now occupied by the city of Cracow was a mostly empty marshland, crisscrossed by many small rivers and streams. The scarce human settlements were to be found in higher, dryer and suitably defensive places. This rather unattractive location had one unquestionable advantage. It sat at the intersection of several important trade routes, meeting here at the ford on the Vistula River. These led from the West to the East – from Germany to Ruthenia, and from the South to the North – from Italy and the Alpine countries to the amber bearing shores of the Baltic Sea. Close to the ford, above the River, there sprung up a limestone hill dominating the area – an ideal location for a ruler wishing to control the surrounding lands. The name "Wawel" was most probably derived from the old Polish word "wąwel", which originally might have referred to a dry bluff rising from a marsh. The convenient location of Wawel was already appreciated a long time ago. The first traces of human presence come from the Neolithic period. In the ninth century, Wawel and the neighbouring Okół (area marked out by today's Kanonicza, Grodzka and Poselska Streets) comprised the heart of the Wiślanie (a Slavic people) state. Towards the end of the tenth century, Cracow was incorporated into the state of Boleslaus the Brave who got rid of the Bohemian garrison stationed on Wawel Hill.

Due to the relations between the Wiślanie State and Great Moravia, as well as to the temporary Bohemian dominion over Cracow, Christianity must have been known here much earlier than in the remaining parts of Poland. There are even some vague information sources preserved pertaining to the first local bishops – Prochor and Prokulf. The episcopacy was formally established in the year 1000, thanks to an agreement between King Boleslaus the Bold and Emperor Otto III. The seat of the episcopacy, and with time also the Cathedral, came to be located at Wawel Hill, commencing the centuries long symbiosis between the religious and secular authorities.

Relics of these ancient times are very scarce, to say the least – traces of earth and timber fortifications and some remains of stone walls. The best preserved church from that time is the Rotunda of the Holiest Virgin Mary (later, SS Felix and Adauctus) incorporated into the walls of the building used in later centuries as the royal kitchens. It might have predated the founding of the episcopacy. There is also the possibility that it was built in connection with the establishment of the Polish Church organization by Boleslaus. The Rotunda, discovered during renovation works in the 1920s, has been partly reconstructed and is accessible as a part of The Lost Wawel archaeological reserve. Clearly recognizable is the central, four leaf layout of the church, and the characteristic split stone wall sections. Comparative studies show that the Rotunda was originally a multi storey structure. The bottom level contained a crypt and the church interior contained an additional gallery for the ruler and his family.

The proper, pre Romanesque Cathedral must have been built around the year 1020, towards the end of Boleslaus the Bold's reign. The remains of its foundations have been found underneath the present Cathedral. Structures relating to functions of the Wawel as the centre of secular power must have existed here at the same time. Built mostly of wood, they left only scarce traces, especially since they were covered up by subsequent structures. Best preserved is the bottom part of the so called "square building" near the northwestern corner of the present courtyard. Recent archaeological studies based on comparative material from Western European countries support the assumption that it was either a storehouse or a treasury.

Much better preserved is the Romanesque phase of the Hill's architecture, though opinions concerning the details of its form and function keep on changing in connection with ongoing archaeological and architectural studies. The Romanesque Wawel began to take its shape in the second half of the eleventh century, after the catastrophic reign of Mieszko II and the transfer of the centre of the Piast State to Cracow. It housed the courts of Casimir the Restorer and Boleslaus the Bold. During Poland's break up into principalities, on the power of the 1138 last will and testament of Boleslaus the Wry mouthed, control of Wawel meant, in fact, the sovereignty over the entire country.

Construction of the Romanesque Cathedral was begun towards the end of the eleventh century, during the reign of Ladislaus Herman. The consecration took place in 1142. It was a three aisled basilica with walls made of uniform cut limestone blocks, with two choirs and at least two towers. The western crypt of Herman's Cathedral, under the invocation of St Leonard, remains to this day. Incorporated into the series of crypts housing the royal tombs, it is also the best preserved Romanesque interior in Cracow. The crypt has three naves covered with vaults supported by monumental columns with cussion capitals. Its architectural details point to the builders' close connection with lands far to the West – on the banks of the Rhine and Meuse rivers. Buried under the crypt floor was bishop Maurus who died in 1118 and whose tomb contained valuables, including a silver missal chalice. Also remaining from the Romanesque Cathedral is the lower part of the Vicar's Tower, also known as the Silver Bells Tower. It is constructed of limestone blocks, the colour and texture of which differ markedly from the Gothic, brick upper sections. The opulence of the Cathedral's Romanesque furnishings can be seen in the impressive bronze handle, shaped as a lion's head, currently kept in the church in Luborzyca near Cracow.

The palace complex – residence of the ruler – stood to the east of the Cathedral. Directly next to the Cathedral, under the northeastern corner of the present Castle, lie the remnants of a Romanesque basilica identified from historical sources as Church of St Gereon. This was most probably the Princely Chapel, but of considerable size with a transept and a crypt. During the period between the demolition of the first, and the completing of the second Cathedral, the Church of St Gereon might have also functioned as a bishop's church. Adjacent to the church from the east was the main fragment of the *palatium*, a large hall of 24 pillars and a residential tower. The defence walls of the Wawel Castle were being expanded throughout the entire early Middle Ages and in particular when hostilities over the Cracow throne began, in the thirteenth century. It should be noted that the Hill was then a closely built town containing other churches, a bishop's residence and other facilities.

The Gothic period brought on deep changes in the construction carried out on Wawel Hill. At the turn of the fourteenth century the whole hill was surrounded with a stretch of powerful stone defence walls. In 1305 a major fire broke out in the Romanesque Cathedral. The old church could not have been completely destroyed, seeing how Ladislaus the Short was crowned there in 1320. The same year, bishop Nanker initiated the construction of the sites' third – and still standing today – cathedral. Its oldest part is the St Margaret's Chapel (now the sacristy). The presbytery was finished in 1346 and the whole church was consecrated in 1364. It is a three nave Gothic basilica with a transept and an ambulatory around the chancel. The side naves and the ambulatory are surrounded by chapels, the largest of which – St Mary's Chapel – is located on the main

axis, right behind the high altar. This layout is based on the cathedral in Wroclaw and also, indirectly, on the architectural traditions of the Cistercian order. The ambulatory and the stone panelling of the interior and on the facade stress the royal status of the Cathedral and are unique among Cracow's Gothic churches. Some of the architectural solutions employed at Wawel, such as pillars with internal buttresses replacing the flying buttresses and the characteristic vaults – based on the triangle pattern, won immediate popularity and became

The tomb of Casimir Jagiellon.

characteristic features of the Cracow Gothic style. Incorporated into the new building were parts of the Romanesque Cathedral – the Crypt of St Leonard and the Silver Bells Tower. The heart of the Cathedral was gradually embellished with numerous additions of various purposes making the Cathedral's Gothic structure hard to read at the first glance. In the fifteenth century, three important elements were constructed. These were the Treasury building, and two mausoleums of the Jagiellonian dynasty – the Holy Trinity, and the Holy Cross Chapels. The recently renovated Holy Cross Chapel in particular constitutes a real treasure trove of late medieval art, as well as a document of the cultural climate in the Jagiellonian state. Its walls and vault are covered with paintings by Ruthenian artists, based on Byzantine models. This is a sign of the great importance of the Orthodox faith in the Grand Duchy of Lithuania, where the Jagiellonian dynasty had its roots. The Chapel is the final resting place of King Casimir Jagiellon and "the Mother of Jagiellonian Kings" – Queen Elizabeth of Hapsburg. The tomb of King Casimir who died in 1492, from under the chisel of Veit Stoss, is among the masterpieces of late Gothic sculpture in Europe. Also found in the Chapel are two late Gothic triptych

The tomb of Casimir the Great.

altarpieces, important examples of the fifteenth century Cracow sculpture and painting.

The above mentioned tomb of Casimir Jagiellon is the last in a magnificent series of Gothic royal monuments, also including the tombs of Ladislaus the Short, Casimir the Great, and Ladislaus Jagiello. All four Gothic monuments are built according to a common template: the dead king, equipped with the attributes of royalty and knighthood, rests on a high sarcophagus which is ornamented with the coats of arms of Polish lands and scenes of the subjects mourning their ruler. Spanned over the king is a canopy symbolizing heaven (the canopy of Jagiello's tomb comes from the Renaissance period and that of Boleslaus the Short from the late nineteenth

century). Typologically, the Wawel royal tombs are based on the Papal monuments in Avignon. Their symbolism, with their complex theological meaning, reflects the late Middle Ages, European knightly tradition. The tombs also present, for the first time in the Polish history, a series of relatively true presentations of the kings' physiognomies. Each of the tombs is also a high grade work of art, illustrating the successive stages in the development of fourteen and fifteen century Cracow sculpture. The series opens with the rather squat sandstone tomb of Ladislaus the Short. The tomb of Casimir the Great reflects artistic links to Vienna. The red Hungarian marble, highly popular in late Gothic and Renaissance Cracow sculpture, was here used for the first time. The Jagiello's tomb is an excellent example of the so called "soft style" from the second quarter of the fifteenth century, and the one of Casimir Jagiellon is a masterpiece of fusing late Gothic naturalism with dramatic expression.

The changes introduced into the Cathedral were accompanied by the gradual expansion of the Castle. A stone residential and defence tower, later called "The Hen's Foot", was built in the northeastern corner most probably at the turn of the fourteenth century. Somewhat later, a new tower was erected in place of the previous Romanesque one. It was the residence of the Danish King Eric during his visit to Cracow and was subsequently dubbed the Danish Tower. Both towers constituted the most presentable part of the Castle and survived to this day. Ground floor of the Hen's Foot is taken up by the magnificent Casimir's Hall, its vault supported by a single pillar. The neighbouring room in the Danish Tower is the so called Jagiello and Hedwig Hall, whose coats of arms decorate the keystones of the vault. Both Gothic interiors now house the Crown Treasury exposition. Equally impressive and well preserved is the exterior architecture of this part of the Castle with the slim oriel of the Hen's Foot and the stone panelling of the Danish Tower. The Hen's Foot complex conveys the idea of the size and magnificence of the Wawel Castle in the Gothic period. It was comparable in size with the Renaissance structure we know today. It also had a similar layout, with wings surrounding the courtyard.

* * *

The Gothic castle on Wawel Hill was destroyed by fire in 1499. The rebuilding, undertaken a short time later belonged to an entirely different era. Apart from the damages caused by fire, the old residence no longer satisfied the needs of the new times. Turn of the sixteenth century was the peak of the power of the Jagiellonian dynasty, ruling not only Poland and Lithuania, but also Hungary and Bohemia and even aspiring to the

Emperor's crown. The construction of the palace – a monument to the powerful dynasty, coincided in time with the great breakthrough in the history of European art, which was the introduction of the Renaissance forms. The construction was decided on by King Alexander Jagiellon. However, his prompt death caused that the majority of the work was carried out during the reign of Sigismund I, later called the Old.

The construction was begun from what is today the western wing. It was erected in the years 1504 1507 as the nearly freestanding palace of King Alexander Jagiellon. The masonry works were directed by master Eberhard Rosemberg, a local builder with roots in Koblentz. The stone elements are the work of an Italian named Francesco, also called Fiorentino after his city of origin (his surname remains unknown). The collision of the local tradition with the Italian art of the Renaissance resulted in compromise solutions, which decided about the shape of the whole Castle. King Alexander's Palace is, in fact, a late Gothic building with a simple ground plan and a steep roof. Following the local tradition and contrary to the Italian custom, the ground floor of the residence was used to accommodate the housekeeping facilities, the first floor – private royal family apartments, and the second floor – also called the *piano nobile* – the staterooms. The Renaissance factor was originally limited to the stone decoration, in particular the oriel window adorned with royal coats of arms and arabesque motives. Built along the same lines were the northern wing of the Castle (1507 1516) and its eastern wing (1524 1529) – the work of master Benedict. The courtyard was closed from the south with a curtain wall by Bartolomeo Berecci (1530 1536). Sections of the old castle, which survived the fire, were gradually incorporated into the new structure. In this way nearly the entire northeastern corner of the Gothic Castle with the Hen's Foot and the Danish Tower were preserved until today.

As the new Palace started to assume its present multiwinged form, the problem of communication along length of the building came to arise, due to the single pile arrangement of rooms. This functional problem led to the most beautiful, and most Renaissance in its nature, element of the Wawel architecture. These are the loggias surrounding its courtyard. The principle of this solution comes from Francesco Fiorentino, who added the loggias to the western and northern wings, the remaining part is the work of Berecci. The loggias of the Wawel Castle draw directly from the architecture of Renaissance Florentine palaces, but specific local conditions forced certain important modifications. No Italian Renaissance courtyard can be compared in size to the Wawel's. The Italians also paid close attention

to geometric regularity of the layout, ignored by the builders here. A specific architectural problem arose at the upper tier of the loggias where the increased height of the *piano nobile* interiors and lack of arcades would require the use of excessively elongated columns. This was solved by master Francesco using a Gothic trick – half way through the height of the columns he put decorative stone rings, which soften the structure's impression of optical instability. Still higher, above the capitals, Francesco placed stone vase shaped elements

The Audience Hall.

in order to free the capitals from deep shadows cast by the protruding roof. Since the courtyard surface was originally lower than today, the slim proportions of the Wawel courtyard were originally even more accentuated. Recent archaeological studies showed that it was once paved in white limestone, similar – at least in colour – to its present renovated state. The remaining architectural elements beamed with colour: – the column shafts were purple, the capitals gilded, and the arcades blue. The Castle roof shimmered with arrangements in glazed tiles. Below the roof ran a brightly painted and only partially preserved frieze, showing the busts of Roman emperors. The Wawel Renaissance Palace took some thirty years to complete. It ranks among the most spacious uniform

Renaissance residences in Europe. The scale of its architecture can be fully appreciated by looking down from the top loggias and – still better from the small attic windows. The recent repairs of the palace roofs pinned their cumulative area at around 6500 square meters. This enormous structure constitutes a specific blend of the Italian models and local requirements of "the Polish sky and custom".

Not to take away from the monumentality of the outer architectural shape, the true splendour of the Jagiellonian

The Audience Hall vestibule.

dynasty was only fully revealed in the Castle interiors. The main element of their original form are the stone portals in the eastern wing, probably made in the workshop of master Benedict. They are an excellent reflection of the spirit of the artistic turning point, their main ornaments being Gothic flutings surmounted by Renaissance mouldings. Most of the chambers in the Renaissance residence of Sigismund the Old share a common decorative pattern. They sit under bare beam or painted coffered type ceilings. The original ones are preserved on the ground and first floors of the eastern wing. The richly decorated ceilings of the *piano nobile* were unfortunately destroyed at the beginning of the nineteenth century and the present ones are twentieth

century reconstructions. Below the ceilings ran painted friezes showing scenes, which inspired the common names of the individual chambers. The original friezes have been preserved in two chambers on the first floor and three magnificent ones on the *piano nobile*: the Tournament Room, the Military Review Room and the Audience Hall. One of the authors of these paintings was Hans Dürer, brother of the famous Albrecht and court painter of Sigismund the Old. The stylistic character of the friezes constitutes a reflection of a significant phenomenon in Polish Renaissance art. While its architecture and sculpture have their origins in Italy, in their finest examples directly from Florence, the painting shows strong links to German art. The walls beneath the friezes were either decorated with textile coverings, or left bare providing empty spaces for hanging paintings and tapestries.

Splendid stoves of colourful glazed tile supplement the whole. They were originally placed along the wall adjacent to the loggia with their outlets leading outside. In this way, the royal chambers were free from the smoke and mess connected with bringing in large amounts of wood and removing ashes. None of the Gothic Renaissance Wawel stoves survived intact. The large stoves, which now adorn the rooms and attract the attention of visitors are Baroque in style and come from the Wiśniowiec castle – today's territory of Ukraine. They play a purely ornamental function nowadays.

The most interesting decorative concept is to be found in the eastern wing Audience Hall. The painted frieze shows human history according to the Greek stoic philosopher Kebes. The coffers of the wooden ceiling were once decorated by 194 wooden, painted human heads by Sebastian Tauerbach and Jan Janda. Only thirty of them survived to this day, and their present arrangement is different from the original one. The Wawel heads are truly mysterious works of art. They are unique in Europe and we do not know what exactly the artists meant to convey. In any case, it is beyond doubt, that such unusual work could not have been merely decorative, but fraught with symbolism.

Decoration of the Wawel interiors was surely subject to some, only partially today understood, ideological framework. It seems to have propagated Christian stoicism, recommending life in accordance with the Divine Order, in virtue and modesty. The Wawel portals still carry stoic adages such as " *Moderata durant"* or *"Velis quod possis".* The already mentioned Kebes based frieze also has noticeable stoic overtones. The same holds true for the heads from the Audience Hall. In spite our gaps in understanding the ideology adhered to in decorating the Wawel residence, its chief purpose was surely to praise the glory and virtue of the ruler – terrible for his enemies, good to his people, wise and pious.

A separate, but essential element of the Renaissance Wawel interior decoration were the royal tapestries. King Sigismund the Old and his wife, Queen Bona had already boasted a rich collection of tapestries, but the real object of Wawel's pride is the collection amassed by Sigismund Augustus. Starting from around mid sixteenth century he systematically commissioned tapestries from the best workshops of Brussels. The whole collection counted 157 pieces, of which 136 survived.

The Wawel tapestries can be divided into three basic groups. The first consists of huge Biblical scenes illustrating the stories of Adam and Eve, the Deluge, and the Tower of Babel. They are in fact grand Renaissance paintings, realized in wool and silk, and richly ornamented with gold and silver thread. The designs are attributed to Michiel van Coxcie, called the Flemish Raphael on account of his close links with Italian art. The second group form tapestries, much smaller in size, portraying landscape and animal motifs. In their attention to realism – to flora and fauna – they also do not differ much from their contemporary painted counterparts. However, it was a specific sort of realism. On one hand it is easy to precisely determine what plant and animal species are being depicted (one of the tapestries even includes the dodo – an extinct bird – in that being an important zoological document), on the other, the same naturalistic approach was used in portraying fantastic beasts like dragons and unicorns.

Finally, the third group contains tapestries with the coats of arms of Poland and Lithuania and the initials "SA" (Sigismundus Augustus) exquisitely framed in Flemish grotesque ornaments.

All of the Sigismund Augustus tapestries are of the highest quality representing the pinnacle of design and craftsmanship. They were of immense value already at the time of purchase. Queen Anne Jagiellon, Sigismund's sister and the last of the Jagiellonian dynasty, donated the tapestries to the Polish state. After the third partition of Poland in 1795, they were shipped off to Russia from were they returned only in the 1920s, revindicated following the Treaty of Riga. They were to hang in the newly renovated rooms of the Wawel Castle for only several years. In the first days of World War Two they were evacuated to Romania and later through France and England to Canada. Along with other objects from the Wawel collection, the tapestries returned to Poland in the years 1959 1961.

The tapestries of King Sigismund Augustus constitute the most precious treasure of the Wawel Museum as the only well preserved element of the residence's original Jagiellonian furnishing. Not only were they a part of the Wawel Castle for over four hundred years, but the majority of them were made specially to fit the measurements of the Wawel interiors. The fact that they are now in their historical place does not ensure they will remain intact for the future generations to admire. These woven paintings are very delicate. It was a fact well known even at the time of their commissioning, and therefore they were displayed in the royal chambers only on special occasions. Even modern conservation methods are unable to alleviate the danger. The natural dyes fade when exposed to light and air pollutants. Internal stress in the fabric, resulting from their immense weight also plays a part. The conservation measures taken do help, but once faded the original colours are lost forever. The only effective way to protect the tapestries from damage is to limit their exposure to light and air. Rolled up and specially protected they may last for a long time to come. That is why we cannot see all the tapestries exhibited at the same time. After all, the future generations have to enjoy them too.

The times of Sigismund the Old and Sigismund Augustus are by far the most glorious periods in the Castle's history and there are good reasons why we have devoted them so much attention. At the same time, equally important events were taking place in the Cathedral. The monumental Renaissance tomb of King John Albert was built by Francesco Fiorentino, as early as 1502 1505. It was the first Italian Renaissance piece introduced into the overwhelmingly Gothic Cracow. It was a real stylistic breakthrough, and at the same time the first example of a new trend in tomb building. The previous freestanding royal monuments were replaced with wall based ones, the architecture of which was based on the classical idea of the arch of triumph. Francesco Fiorentino was an expert in the field of small architecture and stone ornaments. He did not, however, excel in figurative sculpture so the marble slab of John Albert was executed by a local sculptor, still following the Gothic convention. Just like in the Castle, the new Italian trends here intermixed with medieval traditions.

The Cathedral's ultimate Renaissance masterpiece is the Sigismund Chapel, mausoleum of the last Jagiellonians. Its construction was initiated following the 1515 death of Barbara Zapolya, the first wife of Sigismund the Old. The *exemplum sacelli* – a design, or rather a model of the chapel, submitted by Bartolomeo Berecci, was approved by King Sigismund in Vilnius in 1517. The corner stone was laid in 1519 and the finished Chapel was consecrated in 1531. Architecture of the Jagiellonian Mausoleum draws directly from the Renaissance art of Tuscany and Rome. Its analogies may even be found in the drawings of Leonardo da Vinci. The square floor plan, as well as the dome reflect the Renaissance notion of an ideal structure. Berecci's sense of pride in being the architect creator is found reflected in his signature – BARTHOLO FLORENTINO OPIFICE – on the dome lantern, the highest point of the chapel.

Architecture of the Sigismund Chapel shines like a jewel against the bulk of the Cathedral. Its position as the royal sanctuary is stressed by the initially silver dome. In the second half of the sixteenth century, thanks to a

attempt to attribute individual elements to specific artists. The interior of the Chapel is panelled with light grey sandstone slabs. The walls are covered with subtle grotesques and arabesques. Their upper parts present relief ornaments including figurations and the royal coats of arms. The dome's interior is embellished with caissons and rosettes. The royal monuments, made of red Hungarian marble, stand out against this background. The wall opposite the altar contains the joint tomb of the Kings Sigismund the Old and Sigismund Augustus. This

The Potocki Family Chapel – on the right, the tomb of Bishop Filip Padniewski.

sizable donation from Queen Anne Jagiellon, the dome was redone in gilded scale. The Chapel simultaneously contrasts and complements the Gothic Cathedral. Its slender, almost tower like proportions, imposed by its proximity to the tall Cathedral, become truly apparent when looking at its blueprints.

The author of architectural design and of the general scope of the decoration was without doubt Berecci. The opulence of the interior decoration required the cooperation of many highly qualified sculptors competent in the use of Renaissance forms. The team Berecci gathered to realize the royal commission consisted mostly of Italians. Sources give us their names, the contracts however, were signed by Berecci alone. This hampers the

was originally the tomb of the Chapel's founder alone – built in the years 1529 – 1531 to the design and under the supervision of Berecci. In between 1574 and 1575 it was rebuilt by Santi Gucci who divided the niche into two levels, placing the sarcophagus of Sigismund the Old in its upper part and the analogous one of Sigismund Augustus beneath. Gucci also created the tombstone of Queen Anne Jagiellon, which fronts the royal stall.

The Chapel's furnishings equal its architecture and sculpture in magnificence. It should be mentioned that these were mostly the works of Nuremberg artists. The candlesticks and the gilded parts of the magnificent silver altar are the work of Melchior Baier who based himself on the models of Peter Flötner. The altar paintings were made by Georg Pencz and the entranceway grating came from the workshops of Hans Vischer.

It should also be stressed that the artistic whole of Sigismund Chapel was not limited to works in stone, silver and bronze. Following the founder's wishes it also included liturgical music performed by a special college of musicians. This aspect of the Chapel, making it a real masterpiece combining all fields of art, was unfortunately lost in the nineteenth century. The architecture and the décor of the Sigismund Chapel now give a primarily aesthetic impression. It was not this purpose however, that the royal foundation was originally devoted to. It was meant to be a monument to a Christian ruler, executed in accordance with some sophisticated symbolical framework now only partially legible.

King Sigismund was shown as if in slumber, awaiting the final rising at the judgment day. The tomb arcade and the dome make up a double celestial canopy. Keeping vigil at the king's side are: his patron saint, the patron of the Cathedral, of Cracow and those of the entire Church. Quotations from the Bible praise God's supreme glory. These Christian elements are accompanied by accents of antique provenance. Chapel walls are shaped like Roman triumphal arches and in one of the reliefs Sigismund is styled as Alexander the Great. This manner of combining various elements was characteristic of the Renaissance. The Sigismund Chapel décor also includes the before mentioned riddle contained in the mythological scenes embellishing decorating the triangular upper wall sections. We see there sea deities, their legs turning to cloven fishtails, playing (or perhaps fighting) with naked nymphs. What role do these sensual images play inside a Christian chapel – and a royal mausoleum at that? Some scholars interpret it as the artist's foray, quite independent of the king's wishes. They are ready to see Berecci as a humanist, whose outlook bordered on pagan. Another interpretation seeks to "christianise" the mythological scenes and find a way of attributing them meaning befitting the sacral interior. It points out the eschatological function of nereids and the funerary symbolism of the sphinxes, griffins, and dolphins appearing in Chapel reliefs. There is yet another, further going, theory identifying fishtailed creatures as giants and the entire images as examples of *Gigantomachy* – the allegorical battle between good and evil. The controversy among art historians is sure to endure, but the inability to comprehend all the Jagiellonian Mausoleum enigmas does nothing to lessen the impact and our admiration of the masterpiece that is the Sigismund Chapel.

Architecture of the Sigismund Chapel, and the form of the Sigismund the Old tomb, for over a hundred years served as a template for similar works across Poland. The

Wawel Cathedral alone contains several bishops' chapels built on the Jagiellonian model. Dating from about 1530, the bishop Piotr Tomicki chapel is also the work of Berecci. It stands as a simplified version of the Sigismund Chapel, lacking the dome tambour and ornamental sculptures. For that reason it became a direct source from which most of the countless Polish aristocratic mausoleums were derived. The chapels of bishops Gamrat, Maciejowski, and Zebrzydowski date from the mid sixteenth century. The most interesting among them is the chapel of bishop Filip Paniewski (1572 1575). It is a work of Jan Michałowicz, the first Polish artist to fully master Renaissance forms.

The series of sixteenth century bishop' tombs found in the Cathedral is extensive. It opens with the tomb of Cardinal Frederick Jagiellon (1510). Made up of two bronze slabs, it was created in the Nuremberg Vischers' workshops. The Jan Konarski monument (ca. 1521) is already Renaissance in style but the deceased is shown in the traditional pose, lying stiffly on the bier. The bishop Tomicki's monument inaugurates the use of the half prone pose, in slumber awaiting the final judgment. The subsequent monuments have come to illustrate the evolution of sculptural form from classical Renaissance toward the dynamic unease of Mannerism and also provide a good insight into the changing trends in ornamentation.

The history of sixteenth century sepulchral sculpture in the Cathedral concludes at the monument commemorating King Stephen Bathory. This great ruler, through his entire life busy defending Polish borders had no time to think about his own mausoleum. His 1595 tomb, located in the St Mary's Chapel, was funded by Queen Anne Jagiellon. It was created by Santi Gucci and constitutes the pinnacle of Mannerist expressive and decorative tendencies.

* * *

Just like a hundred years prior, two successive fires in 1595, contributed to bringing new artistic style to Wawel Castle. Undertaking the reconstruction, King Sigismund III Vasa employed a new generation of artists working in an austere, early Baroque style. It was the first step towards the Baroque. At the turn of the seventeenth century the royal architect, Giovanni Trevano built the monumental Senators' Staircase in the northwestern corner of the castle. Halls in the northern wing were given new masonry decorations and ceilings. Vaulted chambers were decorated in stucco. The Vasa interiors lost their Renaissance lightheartedness in favour of Counter Reformation severity, fitting the spirit found at the court of Sigismund III. Unfortunately the Vasa wing interiors were seriously damaged by fire in 1702. Their current appearance is the result of conservation and reconstruction work done between the World Wars. The walls were then covered with splendid cordovan – embossed and painted leather panelling. This rare and valuable decorative element, giving the interiors an air of truly royal authority and wealth, is authentic – purchased from the residence of kings of Saxony in Moritzburg near Dresden. The ceilings are made up of oil canvases in richly decorated wooden frames. These were styled after the ceilings at the palace in Podhorce near Lvov. No attempts were made to reconstruct the Baroque paintings. In a brave decision they were replaced by works of contemporary artists.

In 1609, King Sigismund III left Wawel and took up permanent residence in Warsaw. Formally Cracow remained the capital, and the Wawel Cathedral continued to be the place of royal coronations and burials. Nevertheless, the king held court at the Wawel only on special occasions and the, all but abandoned castle, started to fall into disrepair. Serious damages were caused by Swedish troops in the years 1655 1657, and particularly in 1702, when a fire raged through Castle for three days. Out of all the second floor rooms only those in the southern end of the eastern wing – including the Audience Hall – survived. Repair work was begun a few years later with money earmarked for this purpose by the Parliament. Nonetheless, most of the original Renaissance furnishings, including the earlier mentioned stoves were irretrievably lost.

The only positive changes the Castle saw throughout the eighteenth century stemmed from the visit of King Stanislaus Augustus Poniatowski. The Castle acquired then the neo classical first floor reception room located next to the Senatorial Staircase. In the 1790s, the last years of Polish independence, attempts were made at upgrading Wawel's fortifications. The idea was to turn it into a border fortress, as only 100 meters separated it form the Austrian territories laying on the opposite bank of the Vistula River. Recent studies and excavations helped to distinguish this phase of the fortification – including a sophisticated system of gun ports – from the tangle of later additions. Following the third partition of Poland in 1795, Wawel was occupied by the Prussians who robbed the Crown Treasury of the royal jewels. Soon afterwards Cracow fell into Austrian hands, which marked the beginning of the darkest period in the Castle's history.

In marked contrast to the sad fate of the Wawel castle, the Cathedral kept on prospering throughout the seventeenth and eighteenth centuries. The Cracow diocese was still the largest and the richest in the country and the Bishop of Cracow sat in the Senate, next to the Archbishop of Gniezno – head of the Catholic Church in Poland. An important, though not very fortunate modification introduced into the structure of the building was the raising of the ambulatory around the presbytery. Filled with black marble altars and portals, it now gives an impression of a uniform Baroque interior. Sadly gone are its Gothic vaults, and some of the basilical aspects were lost as well. At about the same time, between the years of 1715 1716, the Cathedral Clock Tower acquired the highly decorative late Baroque crowning, attributed to Kacper Bażanka – a Polish architect, who studied in Rome.

The Church interior was also modified with a series of elements designed to provide a suitable ambiance for Baroque religious and state celebrations. These include the gate in the Cathedral wall – designed by Giovanni Trevano, the portal framing the main entrance into the church, the canopy over the St Stanislaus Tomb, and finally the high altar. The most important of them is without a doubt the St Stanislaus canopy. It was built in the years 1628 1630, and is attributed to Trevano. Situated where the main aisle crosses the transept, and constructed of black marble and gilded bronze, it has the form of an open work domed chapel. Due to this arrangement every visitor coming through the main entrance has to climb the high stairs leading to the altar shrine of the Saint – Bishop of Cracow and the Patron of Poland. Obviously not incidental is also the axial alignment of the shrine with the towers of the Na Skałce Church, site of the Bishop's dramatic death, visible through the side entrance. The silver coffin, from 1669 1671, is the work of Peter von der Renner from Gdańsk. It was the most important sanctuary in Cracow. For centuries it has also played the role of a specific *ara patriae* – the national altar for offering trophies won in battles – starting with the banners of the Teutonic Order from the battlefields of Płowce (1310) and Grunwald (1410), to a great banner of Kara Mustapha won in the Battle of Vienna (1683).

Situated in the centre of the church, the St Stanislaus shrine is the focal point of an original Baroque complex, consisting of four tombs of the Bishops of Cracow, set against the Cathedral's four pillars. The first one, that of Marcin Szyszkowski – founder of the St Stanislaus Shrine, was designed by Trevano. It is, however, the tomb of Piotr Gembicki, jointly built by in the years 1654 1657 by the Italians Giovanni Gisleni (architect), and Francesco Rossi (sculptor), that is attributed the highest artistic merit.

Visible through the openings of the St Stanislaus shrine is a classical columned structure of the high altar, built in 1648 1649, most probably to the design of Gisleni. It should be mentioned here that the previous sixteenth century Renaissance high altar, survived to our time, relocated to a church in Bodzentyn near Kielce.

The Baroque period saw a succession of new chapels added to the Cathedral. Standing out from among these seventeenth century additions is the Vasa Mausoleum, externally modelled on the Sigismund Chapel. The Vasa dynasty, which won the Polish throne by the means of a free election, saw it as a way of stressing their family connection to the Jagiellonians. This dynastic propaganda move did not achieve the desired effects. Construction of the Chapel planned already by Sigismund III was began 1664 and not completed until 1676, already after the death of John Casimir – the last of the Polish Vasas. The early Baroque interior of the mausoleum is probably the work of Gisleni.

From among the Baroque bishop chapels, it is important to mention the ones of bishop Zadzik – rebuilt in 1645 1650, and of bishop Załuski – which obtained its final shape in 1758 1766. Most valuable of them all however, is the Lipski Chapel. Its construction progressed in two stages. The first from ca. 1634 includes the building of the tomb of bishop Andrzej Lipski – attributed to Sebastian Sala. The second was done by Francesco Placidi in 1743 1746. He added the monumental tomb of Cardinal Jan Aleksander Lipski and a small presbytery. Its arrangement employs a late Baroque technique of illuminating the altar through a small hidden window. The seventeenth and eighteenth centuries saw many new funerary monuments added to the Cathedral. Instead of reclining figures these were now epitaphs with busts or compositions with kneeling figures, as seen at the tombs of bishops Piotr Tylicki and Andrzej Trzebicki. In the years 1753 1760 Prince Michał Kazimierz Radziwiłł financed the building of tombs for two of his relatives: kings Michał Korybut Wiśniowiecki and John III Sobieski, as well as for their wives. These large structures, embellished with numerous allegorical figures were designed by Placidi and brought to life by the sculptor Mrowiński. The monumental tomb of bishop Kajetan Sołtyk, designed in 1789 by Rev. Sebastian Sierakowski, is made in a similar spirit and pitifully clashes with the Gothic interior of the Holy Cross Chapel.

* * *

The nineteenth century in the Wawel Castle was uneventful from the artistic point of view, still that does not mean that nothing of interest happened on the Hill. The Castle was put to a wide range of uses but mostly as barracks for the Austrian troops. The effects of this were disastrous. At the beginning of the nineteenth

century, the second floor ceilings, including the famous heads of the Audience Hall, were destroyed. The loggias were walled off, which spoiled the architecture of the courtyard for decades, but seems to have saved the weakened columns and arcades. Smaller historical buildings, like the medieval churches of St Michael and St George gradually disappeared from the Hill. In the mid century, after the final annexation of Cracow to Austria, the whole Wawel complex was surrounded by new system of fortifications. Its southern and western sides supported three wings of a military hospital done in a heavy – barrack type – architectural style. On the other hand, the idea of Wawel as the most magnificent monument of national history started to develop among the Poles. The idea of renovating the royal residence came up twice – in 1830 and 1882. Plans were even drafted by the architects Francisco Maria Lanci and Tomasz Pryliński, but never put into effect.

In the nineteenth century the Cathedral gained a number of new and precious works of art. The bishop Padniewski Chapel, transformed in the years 1832 1840 by architect Piero Nobile into the Potocki Family Mausoleum, is a top example of Viennese Neoclassicism. The Chapel boasts an altar painting of the *Crucifixion*, by Francesco Barbieri, a famous seventeenth century Italian painter, sometimes called Guercino, as well as a marble statue of *Christ*, by a leading representative of European Neoclassicism, the Dane, Betel Thorvaldsen. The Potocki family also funded another Thorvaldsen piece standing in the Cathedral, the statue of Włodzimierz Potocki, located in the Holy Trinity Chapel. A thorough renovation carried out in the Cathedral in the years 1891 1910. The works were directed by architects Sławomir Odrzywolski, and Zygmund Hendel, under strict supervision of a committee of historians and art historians. The renovations included supplementing some missing portions of the Cathedral architecture and decoration. Odrzywolski designed new crowning for the Sigismund Tower steeple, and a new canopy for the tomb of Ladislaus the Short. The Treasury and the Szafraniec Chapel acquired polychromies by Józef Mehoffer (1906). The Holy Trinity Chapel was painted by Włodzimierz Tetmajer (1902 1903). Mehoffer also designed the stained glass windows in the Holy Cross and the Szafraniec Chapels. The last royal tombs were added at the beginning of the twentieth century. In 1902, Antoni Madeyski completed the tomb of the Saint Queen Hedwig (Jadwiga), and in 1906, the symbolic tomb of King Ladislaus III. The most consequential aspects of Wawel's nineteenth century history, however, had little to do with either art or architecture, but revolved firmly in the spheres of ideology.

In the nineteenth century, the loss of independence and living under foreign dominion produced a burning need to maintain the divided nation's identity and unity. Cracow, and in particular Wawel became a symbolic place, the treasury and reliquary of the Polish spirit, which had to be kept and cherished. This was the spirit at the stately funerals of Prince Józef Poniatowski (1817) and Tadeusz Kościuszko (1818), whose interment initiated the formation of a pantheon of national heroes – an extension of the royal necropolis. In the 1870s, the Cathedral crypts were adapted to accommodate the growing numbers of tourist pilgrims. The year 1869 saw the re interment of the remains of King Casimir the Great, and in 1890 the ashes of the great Romantic poet, Adam Mickiewicz were brought to the Cathedral. Wawel Hill was connected with the work of the greatest Polish artists. Piotr Michałowski, an outstanding Romantic painter, dreamed of creating a chamber devoted to equestrian portraits of Polish military commanders. In 1882 Matejko donated his painting *The Prussian Tribute* as the founding piece of the future Wawel Museum. The painting's public presentation in 1883, also officially inaugurated the Castle as a museum. Matejko's wish was granted, and his *The Prussian Tribute* – now hanging in the National Museum's Sukiennice Branch – still formally belongs to the Wawel Royal Castle. At the beginning of the twentieth century a plan was put forth by Stanisław Wyspiański, in cooperation with the architect Władysław Ekielski, to transform Wawel Hill into a national "Acropolis". Another artist of the *belle époque,* Wacław Szymanowski planned a gigantic sculpture series – *The Procession of Kings* – to be placed on the building of the former royal kitchens, which would have had to be lowered to the height of the ground floor. Admiration for the boldness and fantasy of these concepts goes hand in hand with relief that they never saw the light of day. Their potential effects on the historical value of Wawel need not even be mentioned.

At the turn of the twentieth century, Wawel was not only the object of bold artistic concepts but also began appearing on a large scale as a motif in literature, first of all in the dramas by Stanisław Wyspiański. The same held true for painting, especially in the work of Leon Wyczółkowski – leading early twentieth century Polish painter. The Wawel Hill served him as a motif for numerous landscapes. The Castle and Cathedral appear – seen from various angles – in countless oils, watercolours, pastels, and lithographs. Today Wyczółkowski's works play a double role as documents and as splendid works of art, executed according to the modern convention in a specific twist on post Impressionism.

In 1905, following long years of effort on the part of the Poles, the Emperor Franz Joseph declared Wawel an Imperial Residence. This allowed for the removal of the stationing Austrian troops from the Hill, and enabled restoration work designed to return the Castle to its original form. The effort was headed by outstanding architects. First by Zygmunt Hendel and later by Adolf Szyszko Bohusz. They conducted archaeological and architectural studies, thanks to which the successive historical stages of Wawel's construction could be retraced. The most famous find was the pre Romanesque Rotunda of Virgin Mary. The First World War did not interrupt the works. They were also obviously continued following Poland's regaining its independence. The task faced by scholars and conservators was immense, both in terms of its scale and difficulty. At stake was restoring the royal splendour of a structure, which for decades served as army barracks, at the same time conforming to twentieth century standards. This meant installing electricity, running water and central heating. A brand new steel roof construction was implemented in 1913. This reduced the threat of fire, and at the same time presented a high engineering achievement. Many elements of the interiors had to be reconstructed based only on surviving fragments or in many cases – like the Vasa wing ceilings – on external sources. Some elements had to be designed anew. Some mistakes were inevitable, as for instance the lowering of ceilings through the use of reinforced concrete beams. This last modification, highly advisable from the point of view of engineering and fire safety, brought on some unforeseen consequences. When the Sigismund tapestries returned to Cracow following the Treaty of Riga, it turned out that the custom made pieces overlap the wall friezes. Their positioning was off by well over a foot, corresponding to the thickness of the new concrete ceilings. It should be remembered however, that at the time of the renovation work nobody knew the exact proportions of the pillaged tapestries, nor even dreamed of them ever returning to the Wawel from Russia. In retrospect, the reconstruction and renovation work done on the Castle by Hendel and Szyszko Bohusz is highly impressive, especially considering the scale and quality of work.

Reconstruction of Wawel was a costly undertaking. Of considerable importance in its financing was the "Wawel Bricks" fund raiser, initiated in 1921. Each donation was equal to a single day's cost of the works. The nation proved to be very generous. Money was coming in from private individuals, institutions, associations and companies. The carefully kept records (published in 1972) speak of over 6300 "bricks". About 1800 of them were presented in material form and embedded in the wall along the course way leading to the Hill from the side of Kanonicza Street (there are some 750 of them today).

In between the two World Wars, the renovated Castle chambers were gradually made accessible to the public as a museum. It was extremely hard to obtain artefacts of proper quality. The great European museums were created in the nineteenth century at the latest, and usually grew out of the rich royal collections gathered

and became a branch of the State Art Collection. At the same time it functioned as a residence of the Polish President. The suite of President Ignacy Mościcki, with all the original furnishing, has recently been made accessible to visitors.

The newly restored independence did not diminish Wawel's position as a romantic monument to the nation's past. On the contrary, this role was expanded. In 1921 Leonard Marconi's equestrian statue of Tadeusz Kościuszko was placed on the so called Ladislaus IV

Wawel in the 18th century (model).

over the course of centuries. Deprived of its statehood, Poland was in no position to amass such collections and the existing ones were largely pillaged during the partition period.

The first major items in the Wawel Museum inventory were objects retrieved from the Soviet Union following the 1921 Treaty of Riga. Many exhibition items were also obtained through donations and as deposits. The museum's policy of foreign purchases should be admired for its foresight and consequence. A collection of Italian Renaissance furniture, gathered in the 1920s, and the 1930s, now comprises the priceless furnishing of the Wawel interiors.

In 1930 the Castle was officially turned into a museum,

bastion, and in 1927 the sarcophagus of the Romantic poet, Juliusz Słowacki was brought to the Mickiewicz crypt in the Cathedral. The solemn funeral of Marshal Józef Piłsudski gathered crowds at the Wawel in 1935. In the following years, the Romanesque crypt under the Silver Bells Tower was turned into his mausoleum. This patriotic gesture, initially opposed by the Church authorities, proved to have enormous meaning in the dark days ahead.

The Wawel Museum had been functioning for only a few years when the outbreak of the Second World War and the German occupation threatened its existence. In the first days of the war its most valuable precious items were successfully evacuated to Romania, from there to

France, Great Britain and finally to Canada. A large part of the collection, however, remained in Cracow and fell into German hands. Wawel became the headquarters of the so called General Government authorities and the residence of Governor Hans Frank. The occupants were preparing to make their stay in Cracow permanent. This turned out for the best, as it spared the Wawel and other historical places from premeditated destruction, like that, which befell Warsaw. The years of Nazi occupation have left a sore stigma on the face of the Hill. The royal kitchens and one of the wings of the Austrian hospital were rebuilt in the spirit of typical III Reich architecture. As seen against the backdrop of ruin and destruction which befell the country in the Second World War, Wawel got off scot free. The damage was limited to an aerial bomb hitting the Eastern part of the Cathedral, the loss of some works of art, and the various Nazi "improvements" to the Hill's architecture. Restoration work started immediately after the liberation. One of the first moves was to tear down two out of the three Austrian barrack buildings. Hardly anyone today is aware of the fact that the fortifications standing next to the Thieves' Tower, as well as the office building hidden behind them are modern creations standing in the place of the now defunct barracks.

In 1953 Prof. Jerzy Szablowski took over the position of Director of the State Art Collection. He kept this position until 1989, and in the meantime was responsible for reshaping and modernizing the Wawel Museum. Since the mid 1950s the Castle saw a major intensification in historical and archaeological studies, connected with the celebration of the millennium of Polish history, in 1966. The respective Wawel exhibitions gradually acquired their present shape throughout the 1960s. The most important and the most frequently visited of these are the royal apartments tour, encompassing mainly the second floor chambers in the northern and eastern wings. Their opening to the public was possible only after the tapestries were returned from Canada. The ground floor of the Hen's Foot, and the adjoining rooms now house the Royal Treasury and the Armoury. Perhaps the most unique part of the Wawel Museum is the Oriental Art Exhibition, which includes a permanent exhibit of Turkish tents. In 1975 a historical and archaeological exhibition – "The Lost Wawel" – was opened in the basements under the royal kitchens building. As before, Wawel continues to perform some official state functions. A visit to the Castle is a mainstay for the various heads of state – politicians and royals – travelling to Poland. Scarce are the VIPs whose signature does not figure in the Wawel Honoured Guest Register.

It goes without saying, that Wawel Hill continues to mean more than just the Royal Castle. Just as it was the case throughout the centuries, the Cathedral continues to be among the main centres of the nation's spiritual life. Its importance grew even stronger through its connection with Pope John Paul II, who for many years held the office of the Archbishop of Cracow. The tradition of the Cathedral as a national pantheon is thriving as well. The toll of the Sigismund Bell always accompanies great religious and state events. The Cathedral is also a unique and world class museum. Apart from the architecture and decorum, it also includes the Treasury. This is the oldest collection of the sort in Poland. The Treasury houses the oldest item belonging to a Polish ruler – the spear of St Maurice given to Boleslaus the Brave by Emperor Otto III in the year 1000. The inventory of similar historical objects is extensive, covering also relics and memorabilia connected with St Stanislaus and St Queen Hedwig. The Cathedral archives boast Poland's oldest and most valuable collection of medieval manuscripts dating back to the twelfth century – the time of the archive's first inventory. Both the Treasury and the archives are available to researchers and the public at large may view an interesting choice of items in the Cathedral Museum.

Jan K. Ostrowski

Birds eye view of the Wawel Hill
(from the north-east).

The arcaded courtyard
seen from above.

Foundations of the St Michael
Church (torn down by the Austrians
in the early 19th cent.).

Wawel Hill in the 18th cent.,
prior to Austrian alterations – model.

The Cathedral, along with its characteristic Clock, and Silver Bells Towers.

The Wawel as seen from the north
– from the site of the medieval *Okół* borough.

The lamb – coat of arms of the
Załuski family – crowning the
Bishop Andrzej S.K. Załuski Chapel.

◄
Figure of St Ladislaus,
seen against the Vasa Chapel dome.

The Vasa
Chapel dome.

The St Leonard Crypt – part of the Romanesque cathedral, dating from the turn of the 12th century, and the final resting place of such luminaries as John III Sobieski, Tadeusz Kościuszko, and prince Józef Poniatowski.

The Classicistic sarcophagus
of King John III Sobieski
in the St Leonard Crypt.

Royal insignia on the coffin
of John III Sobieski.

The sarcophagus of Gen. Władysław Sikorski
– carved from a single piece of Silesian marble.

In front of the sarcophagus
of the Polish national hero,
Tadeusz Kościuszko.

The St Leonard Crypt, with the tomb of Maria Kazimiera (in the foreground), and the
neo-Baroque sarcophagus of Michał Korybut Wiśniowiecki (in the background).

Lid from the coffin
of King Sigismund Augustus.

The Vasa Crypt. Inside,
the sandstone sarcophagus of John Casimir – late 17th cent.

◄

The Holy Father at the St Leonard Crypt, in front
of the altar where he once said his first Holy Mass.

Cross constructed of princely tiaras and the reliquary
containing the arm of St Stanislaus.

The Holy Father saying the breviary
in front of the confession – August
2002. The Mitred Prelate, Janusz
Bielański, kneels next to the Pope.

The reliquaries of Saint Florian, and Saint Stanislaus, exhibited
on the Altar of the Homeland during the Papal visit.

The St Stanislaus confession (shrine containing relics), also called
the Altar of the Homeland – 1628-30.

St Stanislaus with Piotrowin – figure from
the former main altar of the Wawel Cathedral.

The Renaissance main altar from the Wawel Cathedral
– currently in Bodzentyn, near Kielce.

"The Crucifixion" by Peter
of Venice – former main altar from
the Wawel Cathedral.

Women holding up the collapsing Virgin
– fragment of "The Crucifixion".

Former main altar from
the Wawel Cathedral – fragment.

The Wawel Cathedral – main altar,
fragment, 16th cent.

Figure of an angel,
crowning the altar.

The bust of king Ladislaus
the Short – tomb fragment.

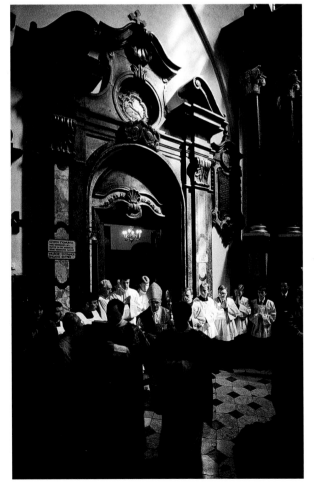

◄
The Ladislaus the Short sarcophagus
– the oldest royal tomb in the
Cathedral, early 14th cent.

Solemn procession leaving the Gothic sacristy
– formerly the St Margaret Chapel.

The head of King Casimir the Great
(red Hungarian marble)
– tomb fragment.

The Cathedral gate, ornamented with the monogram
of Casimir the Great – 2nd half of the 14th cent.

The tomb of Casimir the Great
(14th cent.) – the king's feet
rest atop a lion.

HOC CASIMIRI MAGNI SEPVLCRVM PERACTIS QVINGENTIS ANNIS
A CONDITA AB EODEM REGE ACADEMIA CRACOVIENSI
LEGIBVSVE IN REM TOTIVS REGNIVE VISEICAE SANCITIS
SOCIETAS LITTERARIA CRACOVIENSIS RENOVANDVM CVRAVIT A MDCCCLXIX

The dog at Saint Queen Hedwig's feet symbolises loyalty.

The tomb of Saint Queen Hedwig, carved in Carrara marble – Antoni Madeyski, Rome, 1902.

Queen Hedwig's funerary regalia.

Altar of the Crucified Christ with a Gothic figure
of the Saviour – also called the Black Cross of St Hedwig.

The head of King Ladislaus Jagiello rests on two lions, symbolizing greatness, and might.

The tomb of Ladislaus Jagiello – red Hungarian marble, surmounted by a Renaissance sandstone canopy.

◄
Tomb of Casimir Jagiellon in the
Holy Cross Chapel – Veit Stoss (1492-94).

Veit Stoss carved the king's head
in spotted Salzburg marble.

The Holy Cross Chapel – triptych altar
to Our Lady of Sorrows (end of 15th cent.).

The Holy Cross Chapel – Gothic Holy Trinity Triptych – splendid
specimen of late medieval Cracow sculpture (1467).

The Assumption of the Holy Virgin Chapel (also called the Sigismund Chapel)
– tiered tomb of Kings: Sigismund I the Old, and Sigismund Augustus.

The figure of Sigismund the Old
– the Sigismund Chapel.

The head of Anne Jagiellon
– tomb fragment (by Santi Gucci, 1574-75).

Sigismund Chapel – the head of King
Sigismund Augustus (tomb fragment).

Cartouche with the white eagle
of Poland – Sigismund Chapel.

Cartouche with the white eagle of Poland
– tomb of Anne Jagiellon.

The Silver Altar
– Dormition of the Virgin.

The Silver Altar – Old Symeon holding
the Baby Jesus (the Offering panel fragment).

The Silver Altar
– the Briss scene.

The Mocking.

The Silver Altar
– the painted Crucifixion panel.

Jesus judged
by the high priest.

The Silver Altar
– Christ's Burial.

The head of King
Stephen Bathory – red marble.

The Holiest Sacrament Chapel (also called the
Bathory Chapel) – the altar.

White marble figure of Christ – tomb
of Count Artur Potocki (by Bertel Thorvaldsen).

The Crucified Christ – gilded bronze
altar in the Absolution Chapel.

◄
The St Thomas of Canterbury Chapel – tomb figure of the chapel founder,
Bishop Piotr Tomicki (by Bartolomeo Berecci).

The Konarski Chapel – tomb figure
of Bishop Konstanty Felicjan Szaniawski.

The Holy Trinity Chapel – white marble figure of Włodzimierz Potocki
styled as an ancient warrior, by Bertel Thorvaldsen (1820-30).

The Passion Chapel (also called the Czartoryski Family Chapel)
– neo-Gothic triptych with late Gothic figures.

Pearl-studded chasuble – gift
of the Cracow Voivode Piotr Kmita, 1504.

Reliquary containing a nail from the Holy Cross
– 1st half of the 18th cent.

The Spear of St Maurice
– presented by the German Emperor
Otto III to Boleslaus the Brave, during
the year 1000 Gniezno summit.

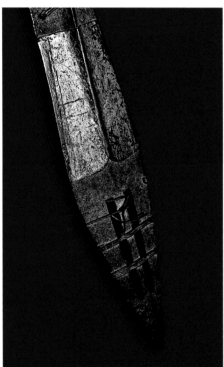

Reliquaries containing the head and arm
of St Stanislaus – the Cathedral Treasury.

Toll of the Sigismund Bell accompanies
the most significant national and the Church events.

The word "Wawel" used to mean
a dry bluff rising above a-bog.

◄
Wawel Hill – perfect location from
which to govern a vast territory.

Each new breathtaking view
affords fresh impressions.

◄
The pre-Romanesque Holiest Virgin Mary Rotunda (under the invocation
of Saints Felix and Adauctus), was originally a two-level structure.

The Rotunda's apse
– fragment.

Romanesque column from the
St Gereon Church – fragment.

The Holiest Virgin Mary Rotunda was
discovered during archaeological excavations
prior to the First World War.

The Holiest Virgin Mary Rotunda at the "Lost Wawel"
archaeological reserve – fragment.

Plaque at the entrance to the Holiest Virgin Mary Rotunda,
describing its history and reconstruction efforts.

Turret containing the staircase down
to the Dragon's Den.

Cobblestone street, between the Senators'
and Sandomierska Towers.

► The castle gateway
and the Sandomierska Tower (15th
century) – also called the Bernardine
Tower – as seen from the Senators' Tower.

The Sandomierska and Jordanka Towers
– view from the hotel "Royal".

The Hen's Foot and the Danish Towers
– left over from the Middle Ages.

Construction of the courtyard was directed by Francesco Fiorentino, master Benedict and Bartolomeo Berecci.

Renaissance arcades.

An eagle from the time of Casimir the Great over the gate leading into the residence.

The
Vasa Gate.

A tapestry from the "Life of Noah" series – Noah with his wife before boarding the Ark.

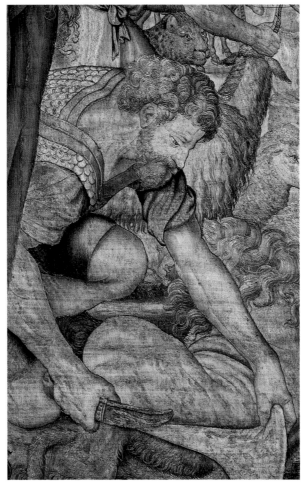

◄

A fragment of a tapestry from the Senators' Hall – Noah's sons embarking the Ark.

A tapestry from the "Life of Noah" series – Noah offering a sacrifice of thanks.

The mysterious heads were sculpted
in the 1st half of the 16th century.

Restored heads
before being remounted in the coffers.

The Birds' Room
– as it used to look.

Vestibule joining the Eagle Room and the Birds' Room
(former dining chamber of Sigismund III).

The Eagle Room.

◄

Part of the vestibule
leading to the Senators' Hall,
with the portraits of kings: Michał Korybut
Wiśniowiecki, John Casimir Vasa,
and Constance of Austria.

A 17th century
Turkish tent.

89

The Dutch study
in the Sigismund III Vasa Tower.

A chapel on the second floor – adjacent to the Birds' Room. An image
of the Resurrected Christ on the altar.

The Zodiac Hall.

A pine cone shaped vase – majolica faience,
Deruta (Italy) ca. 1520.

The Planet Hall. On the right, a tapestry
showing a unicorn-giraffe creature.

A travel chalice and paten,
mid 11th century.

Fragment of an exposition
in the Casimir Room.

▶
Missal chalice
– commissioned in 1507
by the Breslau canon, Appicius Colo.

Cups made from coconut shells, 17th century.

A tray featuring aquatic deities, Augsburg, masterpiece of the Elias I Drentwett workshop, ca. – 1630.

▶

An epergne featuring the coats of arms of Sigismund III Vasa, 1600.

The Lanckoroński gem
– Byzantine masterpiece,
6th or early 7th cent.

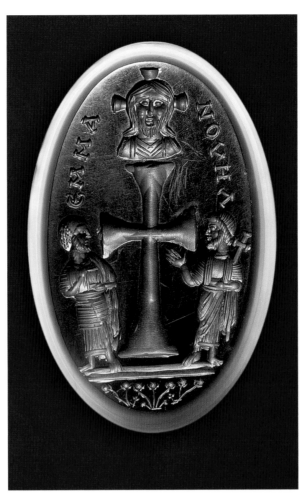

◄
A multilevel, winged home altar made in an Augsburg
workshop – early 18th cent.

Chalices
– Germany, 16th-17th cent.

A decorative chest
– early 17th cent.

Coronation slippers
of King Sigismund Augustus.

Decorative buckles
– Transylvania, 17th cent.

An Augsburg jug by H. J. Baur (1630), and a Nuremberg stein, from the workshop of A. Treghart (ca. 1620).

Ship-styled cups from the workshop of Esaias zur Linden – early 17th cent.

Cannons and banners taken in the battle of Grunwald,
exhibited in the cellars of the Hen's Foot Tower.

Tournament armour – workshop
of Konrad Poler, Nuremberg, ca. 1490.

Tournament masks
– 16th cent.

Fragment of a Hussar
armour breast-plate.

Star of the White Eagle Order,
on plate type armour.

Western-European helmets
– 16th cent.

Western-European
armour.

Hussar armour
– 17th cent.

Hussar armour
– 17th cent.

Battle flails and a mace.

Parade rapiers – 16th and 17th cent.

Pole arms
in the armoury vestibule.

Crossbows:
top – Renaissance, 1541;
bottom – Baroque, 18th cent.

The sword given to the Cossack Hetman
Piotr Konaszewicz Sahajdaczny, by King Ladislaus IV.

Kalkhan – round,
Oriental shield – 17th cent.

Saddle belonging to the Wojnicz Castellan, Przecław Szembek
– trophy taken in the battle of Vienna (Turkey, 17th cent.).

The sword of Sigismund the Old,
early 16th century.

The Crown Treasury, *Szczerbiec* (The Notched Sword)
– coronation sword of the Polish kings.

The
Thieves' Tower.

The Tadeusz Kościuszko
monument, by Marconi.

The Cathedral and gardens
– view from the south.

▶
The Sandomierska Tower
in springtime.

The Clock Tower
surrounded by trees.

The
Wawel gardens.

The Hen's Foot, and
the Sigismund III Tower.

The Silver Bells Tower
amidst lush vegetation.

The Clock Tower
cloaked in snow.

Christmas
at the Wawel.

Winter – a view from
the Dębniki district.

NEW VERSION OF THE ALBUM
"WAWEL – THE CATHEDRAL AND CASTLE"

Editing and publishing concept
Leszek Sosnowski

Editing co-operation and captions
Jolanta Sosnowska

English translation
Eunika Bogucka-Jamka
Tom Chwaja

German translation
Jolanta Lenard
Language consultant
Otto Riegler

DTP
Biały Kruk Studio
Janusz Feliński
Patryk Lubas

Proof-reading
Bogdana Kłeczkowa

Printed in Czech Republic

© Copyright by Biały Kruk Sp. z o.o.
Wszelkie prawa zastrzeżone
All rights reserved

Biały Kruk Sp. z o.o.
ul. Szwedzka 38
PL 30-324 Kraków
Tel./Fax: (+48) 012 260 32 40,
012 260 32 90, 012 260 34 50
e-mail: biuro@bialykruk.pl
www.bialykruk.pl

First edition
Cracow 2006
ISBN 83-60292-17-5